Sacred
Beauty Coloring Book

Copyright: Published in the United States by Peter Raymond
Published August 2018
ISBN-13: 978-1724789259
ISBN-10: 1724789252

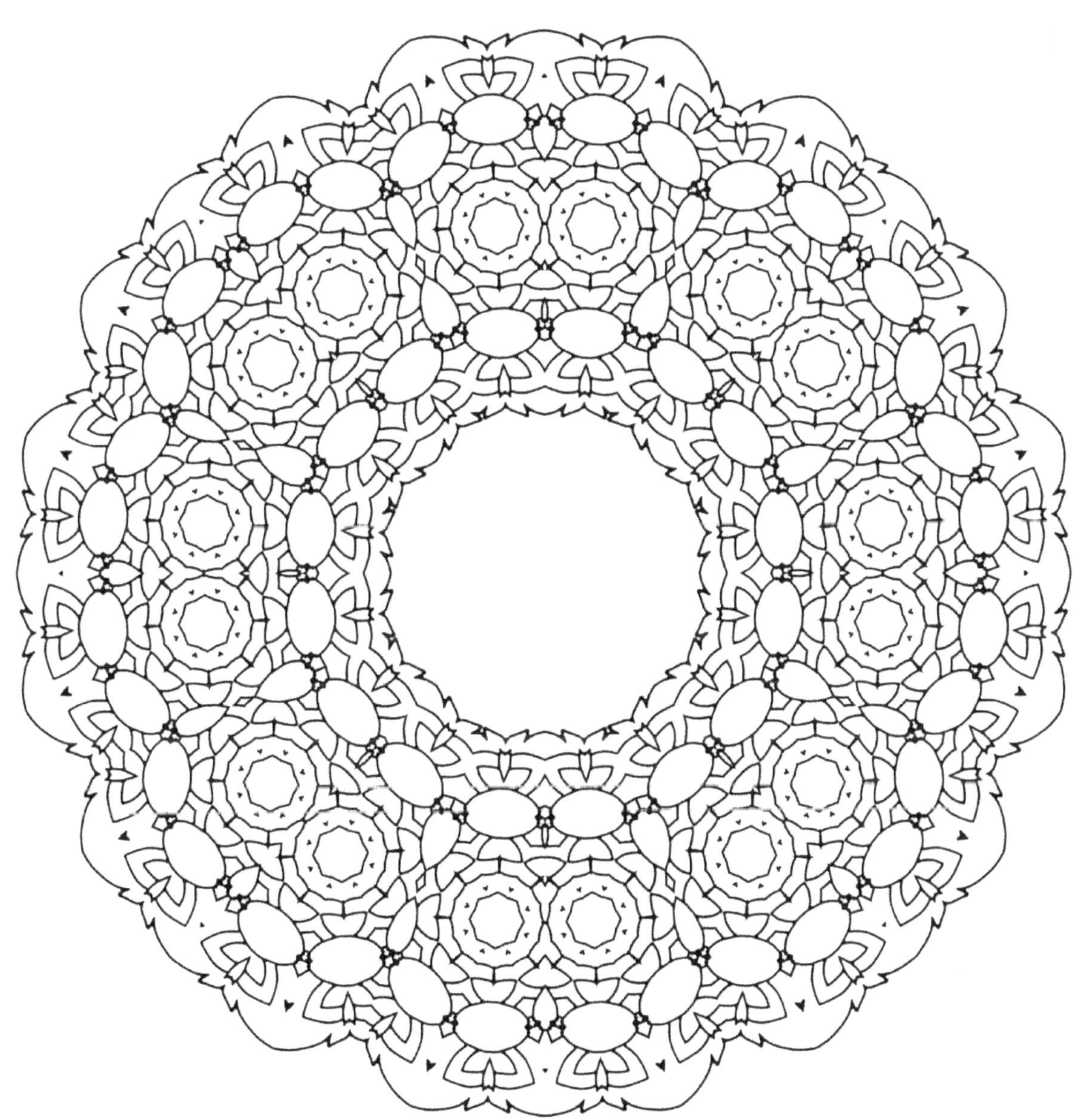

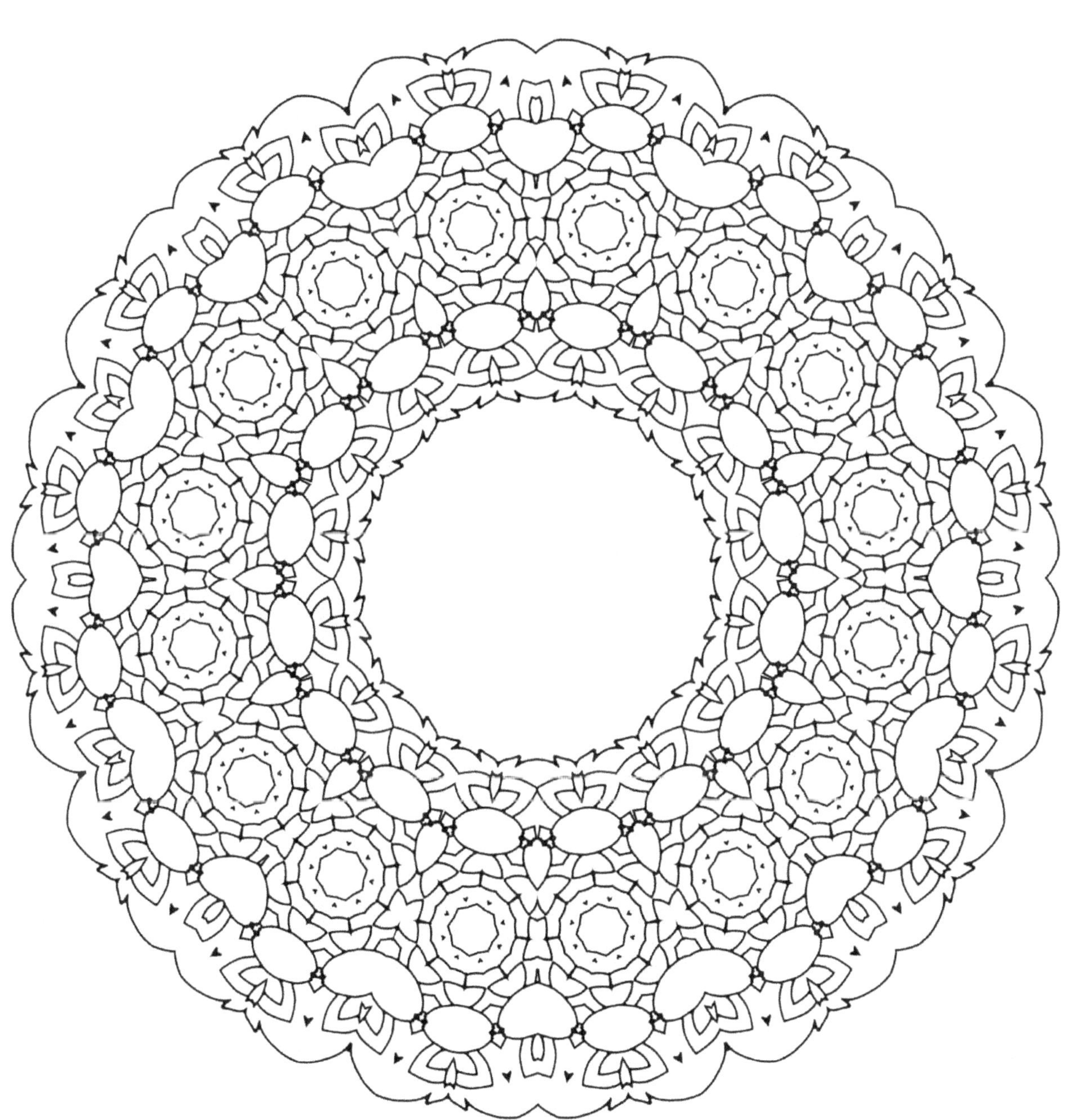

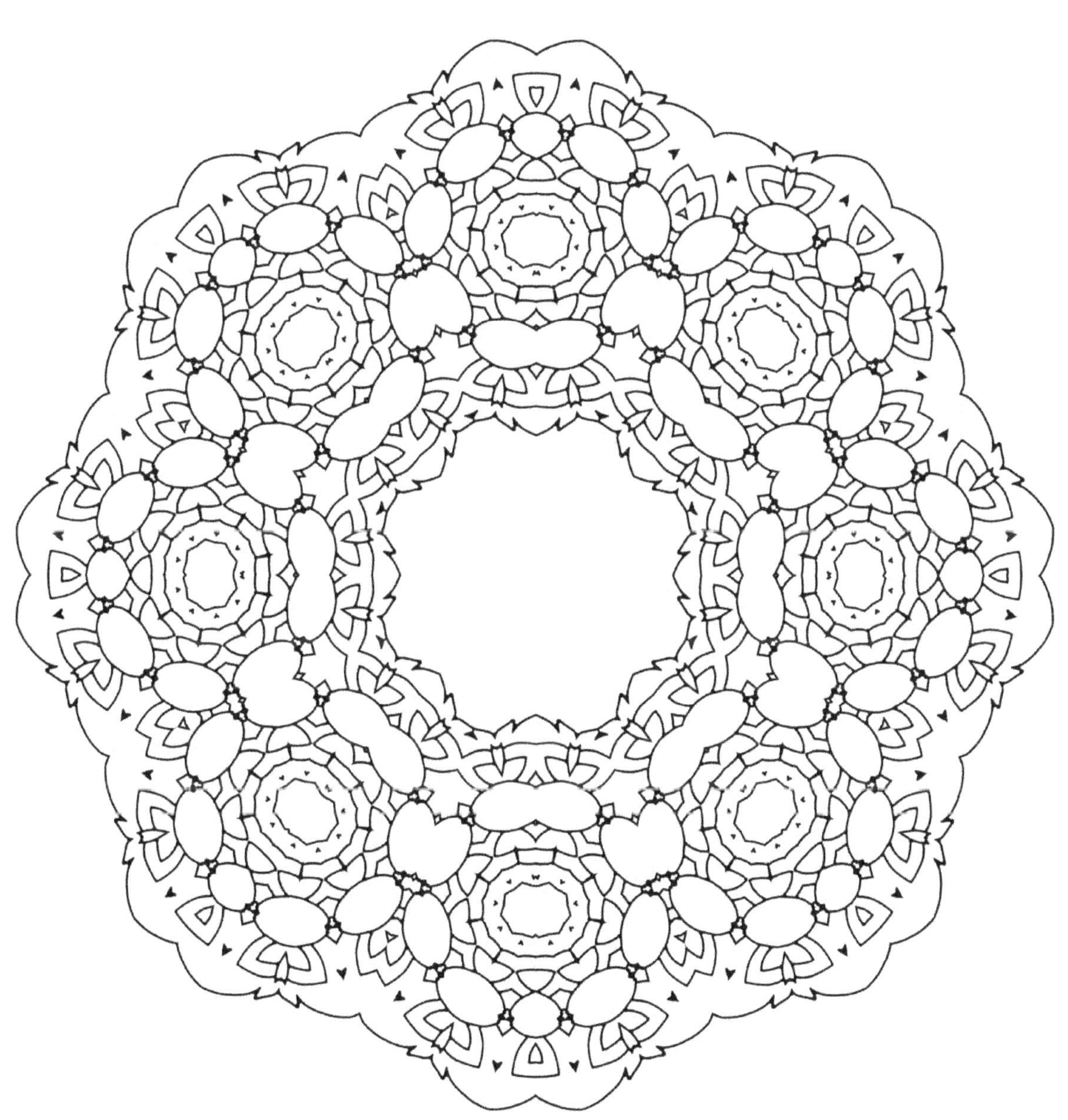

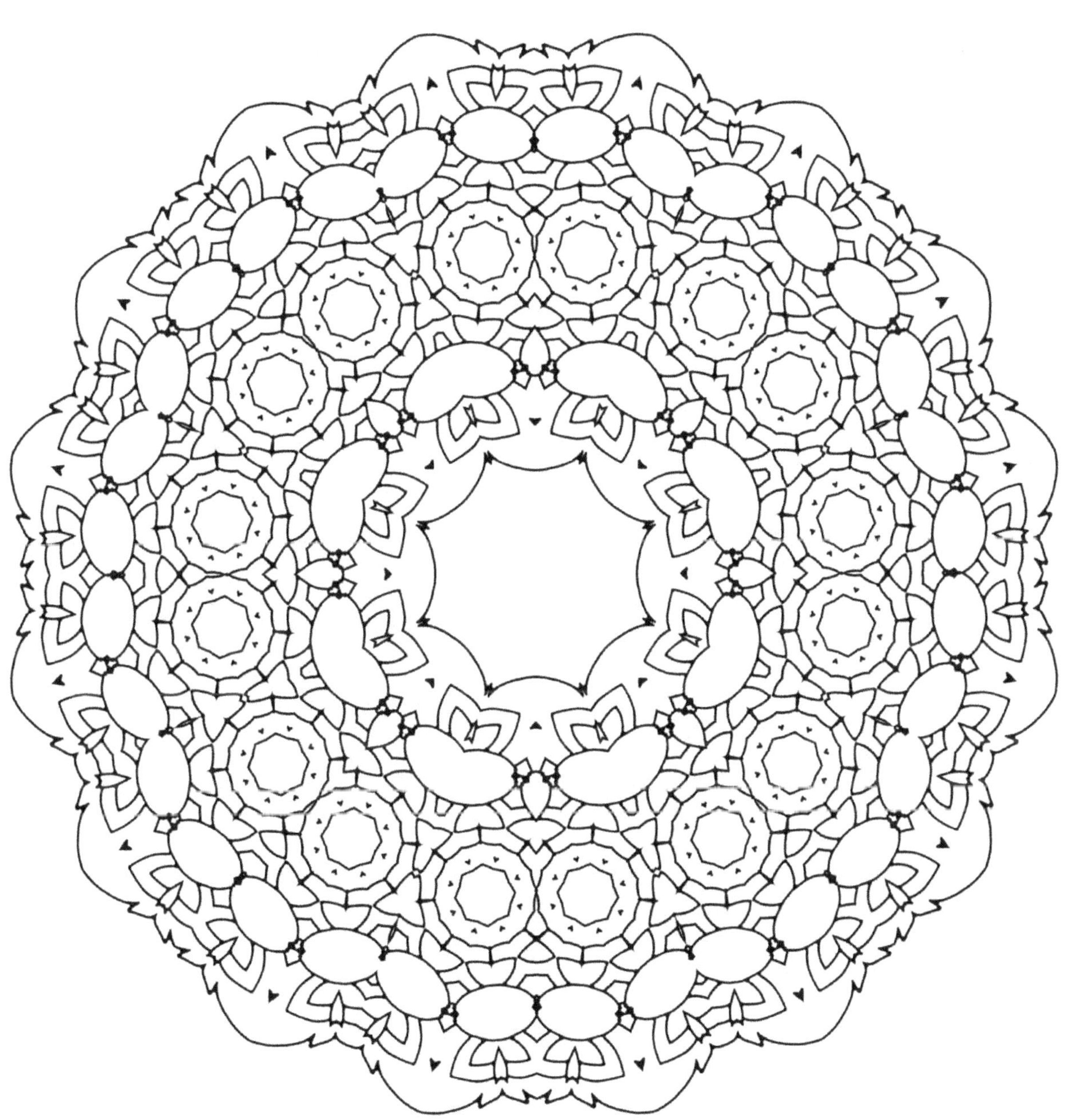

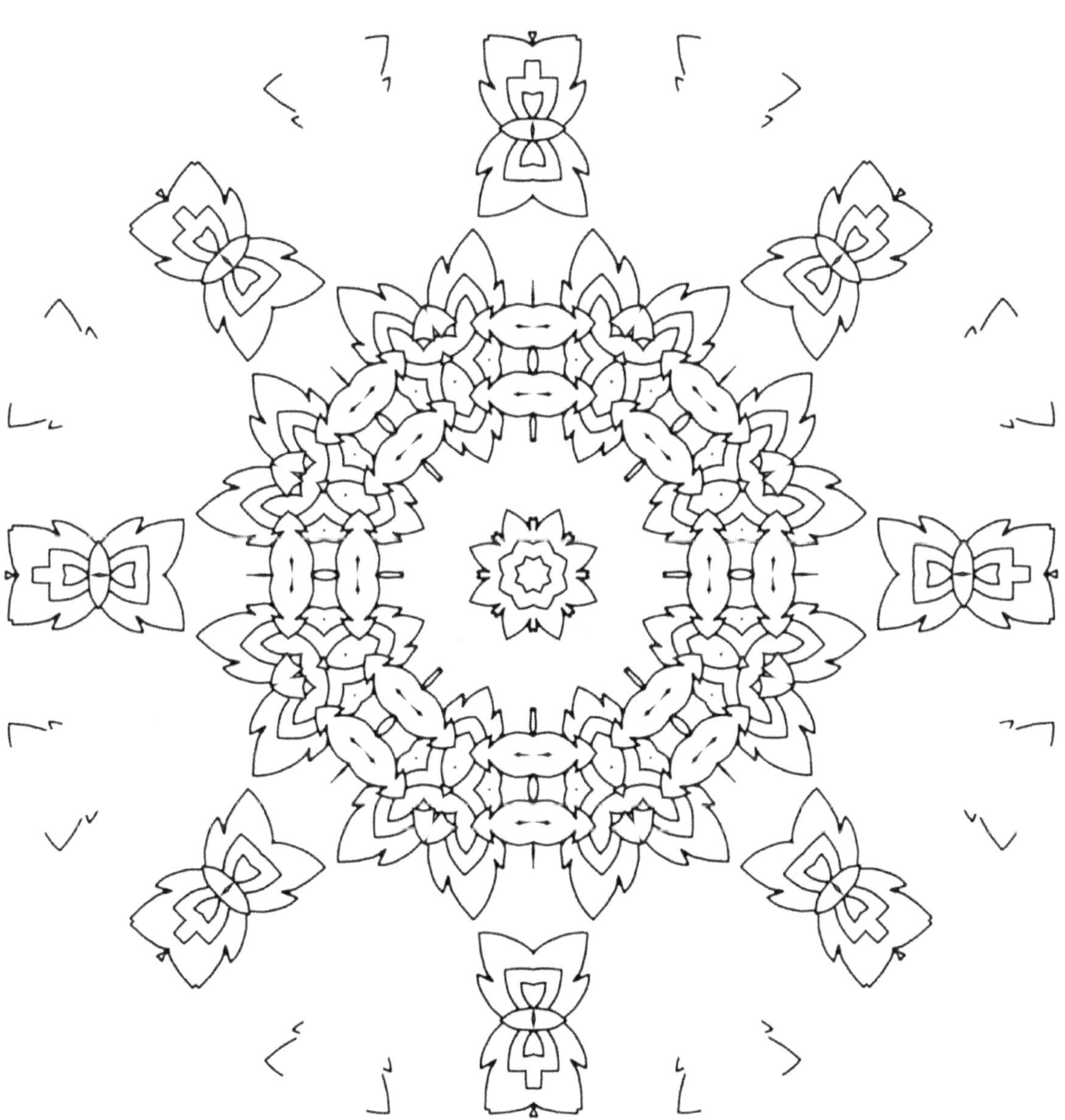

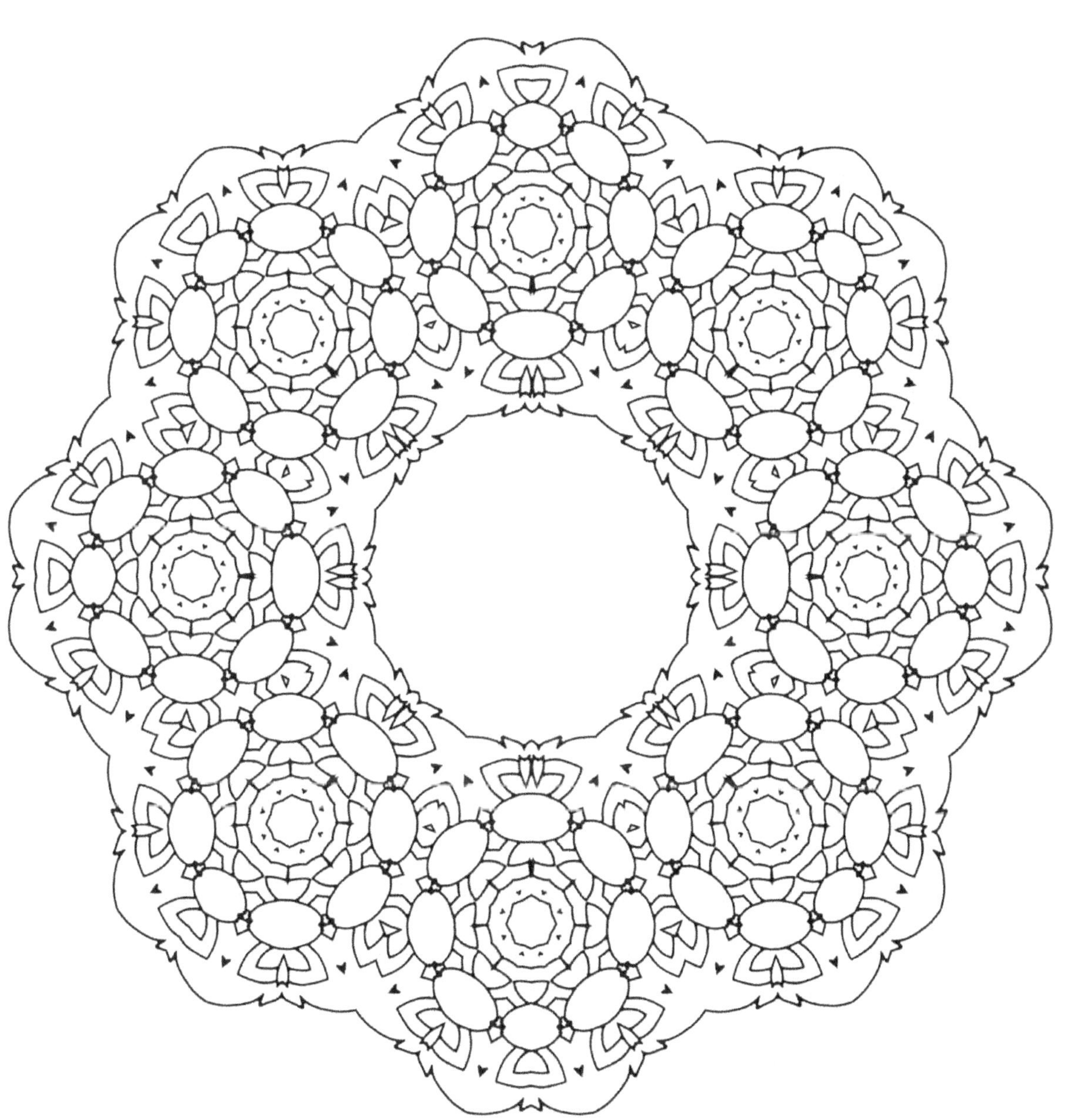

Thank you